Along the Side of the Journey

Jorge González Moore

Along the Side of the Journey

Jorge González Moore

EDITORIAL JGGM

ISBN 978-958-46-4441-1

Copyright © Jorge González Moore, 2013
ALL RIGHTS RESERVED

Original title in Spanish: A la Orilla del Camino
First Edition in Spanish: May 2013
First Edition in English: May 2014
Aberdeen, Scotland, United Kingdom.

Edited and published by **Editorial JGGM**, May 2014
j.gonzm@hotmail.com
jorge.gonzalezmoore@asu.edu

Design: Eduardo Forero Ángel
Photo-mechanics, printing and binding: **Editorial JGGM**
Printed in Bogotá, Colombia, May 2014

No part of this publication may be reproduced, stored in or introduced into a retrieval system, or transmitted, in any form, or by any means. It is not allowed its reproduction, transmission or storage of the whole or part of this work, including the design of its cover, its inside, pictures, cartoons and/or illustrations, its editorial logo, nor is it allowed its informatic/computerized treatment, in any form, by any means or process, including electronic, electrical, mechanical, chemical, optical, recording, photocopying, by register or otherwise, and its translation into any language, lease, rent or any other form of transfer or cession of this work/creation without the prior written authorization of the author.

*For all those,
that without expecting anything in return,
strive to make this world
a happy place*

*and to my readers,
for believing that it is possible.*

Acknowledgments:

To my family, friends and readers
for your generosity
and for joining me on this journey.

Aberdeen, Scotland, United Kingdom, 2013.

Foreword:

We are full-time travellers. Tourists advancing through extensive paths opening at our feet. Through uncertain and dazzling trails. Across immeasurable distances and times. We anxiously travel to a destination that welcomes and shelters us, and gives us a break on this extensive and hard journey. That provides the calm to not continue moving forward. A destination that shows us that we have arrived, that after so much travel we have stepped to the mainland; that the road is finally over and we can rest.

But as many miles that we walk or centuries that have passed, no matter how much we struggle and we run, no matter how misleading is the mirage in the desert, that distant point on the horizon does not appear, and it is hard to understand that we will never arrive.

Because we are just walkers, and therefore, our destiny is in the trip itself. It that, that we carry along and accompanies us. In that, it gives us breath. It is what caresses our face in every step and makes us look occasionally along the side. To understand that the distant point we never saw has always been along our side. Joining us in every fall and every breath, every pain and every joy, filling us with strength and enriching adventures, because what matters is not our fate, what matters is what is **along the side of the journey.**

There is where the magic lies.

There is where we must search.

Carlos Esteban Orozco Posada
Bogotá, Colombia, 2013.

Introduction:

In this third book I am consolidating the evolution of my literary concept,
to contribute in a modest way to literature,
that consists in
the use of the space itself
as the structure
upon which the text is constructed
and the reading should be done.

Each phrase or thought,
is consciously deployed on the page as fragments
and the space is a grammatical component
and a writing resource as well
that generates pauses and moments for reflection necessary to transmit
and get the message understood based on an initial idea
followed with a sudden change or circularity
among other mechanisms.

My objective is that the thought is read and internalized
in a more powerful and purposeful way
unlike to when the same idea is posed
with the text unbridled in the space
and in which grammatical signs are not enough to express
the sense that I want to deliver.

In turn
each phrase is part of an infinite
a cosmos of possibilities of ideas and experiences.

I think literature should be perceived with as many senses and means as possible,
and here is a contribution that generates a different way
using the universe that is the page
to model the wording within that space-time
which is the page-reading.
I used this concept and scheme
to build the prose of this introduction.

In the area of poetry
I did an experiment with the poem "Premonitions"
which can be read in order from beginning to end,
as from the end to the beginning,
finding new messages and melodies.

I hope you like these concepts
and this new book.

Aberdeen, Scotland, United Kingdom, 2013.

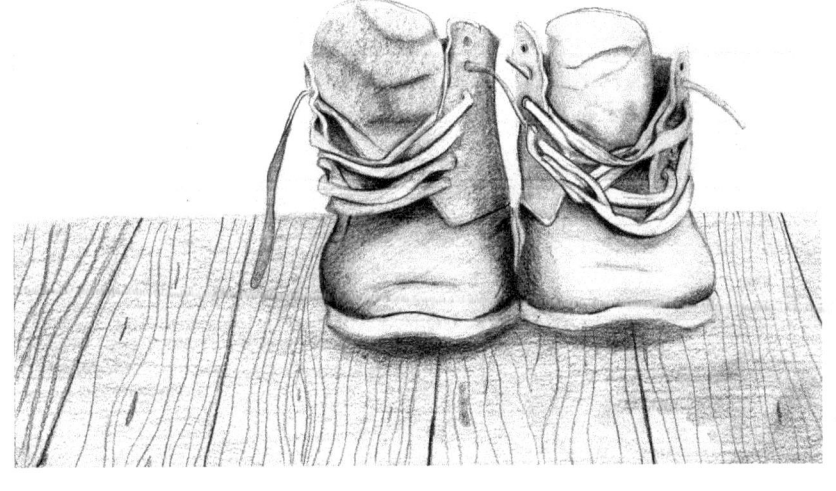

THOUGHTS AND REFLECTIONS

Living the unsurpassed fortune
to enjoy life being true,
with hope for the future,
surrounded by people who love us
and we are delighted to love.

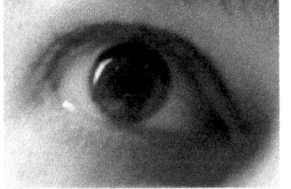

I. Paths

Wise is the one who manages to build sustainability.

We know who the individual is because of his or her fruits.

The truth simplifies.

When confronted with their own image,
people with a flawed character always conclude
that the defective must be the mirror.

With the power to be a prophet of the extraordinary
and the catastrophic, most choose the latter.

The citizen must remember
more his or her duties than his or her rights.

Death touches us all. It is just a matter of time and place.
It is useless to resist the inevitable,
but where there is hope there is a chance for life.

What served us in the past does not serve us now,
this is why we must be flexible and fluid
to continuously adapt.

What wears the most from a disease
is the relentless exhaustion that it produces.

The total devotion to a single moral value
triggers tragedy.

The war between nations leads to disgrace,
but the civil war within a nation produces ruin
as it divides families and friends.
The post-civil war peace is fragile
consequence of its participants´
hatred and revenge.

I think that the closest thing to purgatory
must be being a patient
in a hospital´s emergency room.

Who misses the most
for being incapable to listen to others
is one self.

It is easier to beat the opponent by exhaustion than by fighting.

The biggest challenge of a leader is his or her own character,
as well as learning to doubt of his or her pride and instinct
to change his or her thought perspective.

Not showing doubt is a sign of conviction
as well as of foolishness.

In the web that is our life
we must bear in mind that it depends
more than we would like,
of the actions and inactions of others.

There are very successful people when it comes to failing.
There are even some determined to fail.

All vice is a habit, but not all habit is a vice.
The good habit is routine and discipline.

Change occurs if it is the organization's base
who understands and executes it.

The constant in underdevelopment is the fear
and inability to assume commitments.

Life is a bet.

It is easy to talk about values
when not living in the raw reality.

The best inspiration to write is to read.

Do not trust on the ease and conviction
given by abstraction.

Proper reflection considers,
feels and weighs all the consequences.
Nothing further from fanaticism
than proper reflection.

There is no time for fear.

If politicians kept their promises
then since immemorial times
the world would be a dream.

A leader is affectionate to responsibility.

It is sad to change one's master without realizing
that we are still slaves,
with luck at least we are free
to choose our master.

People forget the basics, that war ends
only winning it.

The journalist has become a judge
with a communication media as guillotine.

Some people use their memory
just to torment themselves.

Bad luck is irresistible.

Life is a controlled accident.

The closest thing to love is faith.

Resentment has been the fuel
of the greatest savages in history.

Who distrusts others has no surprises,
except when others treat him well.

We learn to appreciate things
when we understand that the other
helps us without obligation.

Globalization is as new as the first empires.

Women like men to direct them
exclusively on what they want to be directed.

The seed of opinion
has intelligence as its fruit.

Life is a gamble in which we have
the option of loading the dice slightly,
at least in part it obeys our decision.

Thinking about what does not corresponds
is the spark that ignites misfortune.

In the end, individual goals may change in time because of the individual motivations. Sometimes it is not about who has the resources but who has the drivers to keep on going against all the odds. Nevertheless, reality beats all that, and if you do not entirely understand what you are up against, no plan is going to work. All things been said, nothing is certain and that is why risks must be taken.

Success is to know what to do and doing it.
A mistake is to know what to do
and don't do it, hence destroying value.
Failure is not knowing what to do
and doing something else
that destructs even more value.

Clumsiness is a human quality,
animals are never clumsy.

Suffering does not make anyone just.

It is always a historic moment.

The most uncomprehended is reason.

Moments and things depend on who we share them with,
the same time and thing can be joy or tragedy.

The problem with war
is that once everybody is dead
survivors can feel lonely.

The most effective and fast form of communication
is panic.

A large part of life is required
to be able to do what you want and then you can not
because you have to spend the rest of your life
setting a good example.

A secret that involves more than two people
ceases to be.

Good manners are profitable.

What is it that life strives to teach in every moment
if not prudence.

Politicians are experts at evading reality.

The hardest thing to hide is affection.

We are slaves of our irresponsibility
and victims of our responsibility.

Happiness is proportional to autonomy.

The purpose of a leader is to create extraordinary teams.

Once the events occur everybody starts pondering
that the antecedents were premonitory.

The worst decisions are those
taken based on circumstantial arguments
in order to solve structural issues.

The wise men and fools are alike
because none learn from their mistakes.

We are accomplices of our reality.

With delirious enthusiasm the people celebrate
the elimination of their rights.

The victors often have
many allies and friends.

Our decisions should lead us where we want to arrive.

When we are stubborn to understand reality
there are no signs nor reality worthwhile.

My intelligent moments occur
when I listen to others without prejudice.

The problem with experience
is not only that it teaches very slowly
but also teaches both good and bad habits.

Leadership must be strategically pragmatic
and pragmatically strategic.

Seek to be autonomous on what is important
and dependent on the trivial.

You can reason with the inadequate
as you can reason with cancer.

Good design's most important resources
are intelligence and good taste.

Although it does not seems like it, what makes a happier existence
is the innate ability to forget.

The difference between what is and should be
is directly proportional
to the misery and unhappiness of a society.

Bad luck: Adding bad will to something already going wrong.

We are all slaves of our mortality.

Having no North
dims intelligence.

Helping would be easier if aid recipients
were aware of the effort done by those who help.
Subsidies do not work as the recipients
do not understand that these are not free.

Populist and corrupt politicians are the first to wish
that poverty expands to perpetuity.

Marriage consists in the willingness
to stay married.

Those who end up educating a man are his wife and children.

Life is made of the small things.

What a delusion to believe that recursiveness compensates defects.

The problem of defects
is that they increase over time.

A better world is made by preferring responsibility
over tranquillity.

Nothing more unfair and profane
that injustices made in the name of justice.

In life you have to be resourceful
at least to make new mistakes.

There is nothing more inefficient than to do well
what did not have to be done.

There is not so much shame in the officials' we have
as in the voters who elect them.

The bad journalist is detestable
because it usually takes as his or her own
the successes of others, who he or she was unwilling to support
when they were battling to emerge.

The theory of the exercise of certain rights is just theory,
as is the case of many obligations.

The problem of citizen's discipline
is that when there are hordes of disobedient citizens
nothing can help impose order.

The bad journalism has the sad effect
of legitimizing the inadequate.

The static perfection does not exist
because its spirit is evolution.

Excuses is what humanity needs
to initiate the great transformations.

Beware of those who in name of democracy
shut down all opposition.

Regarding underdevelopment, the problem
is that since arriving to the country it is felt,
and not so much because of the poor infrastructure
but because of the underdeveloped attitude and thinking:
the treatment in question.
Not even do they collude to make believe otherwise.

The truth does not tolerate ornaments,
lying; all.

For useless things, just one is enough.

We must struggle to not be defeated
by our own haste and tiredness.

The secret of happiness;
increasingly sticking to people
and less to things.

Sometimes I think I need a vacation from myself.

Hell must be like
trying to build our own home
with unreliable contractors.

The true social equity
is based on a real opportunity to access justice.

The fact of getting married means that now two women will
scold you;
your mother and your wife.

In developing countries
it is most notorious the fact that governments
do not legislate what is of interest to people
as much as that of interest to the bureaucrat.

From a hurry not only fatigue should come,
at least the satisfaction
of having arrived in time should remain.

Respect and trust
are the foundations
of a healthy relationship.

Inflation is the most subtle and efficient thief.

It is terrible that the vast majority of injustices
happen because of frank indifference.

Creative destruction makes capitalism
the only constant revolution.

It is not that some politicians and journalists lie,
it is just that they try to avoid the truth at all cost.

Public opinion and general criteria
is made especially by those
who have neither the first nor the latter.

The revolutionary says that before the revolution
man was subjugated by man,
what the revolutionary avoids saying
is that after the revolution
man really subjugates man.

Nothing is more subjective than journalism's objectivity.
The journalist vehemently reports in a subjective way
what he or she does not know.

A true patriot is closer to the truth
than to his or her homeland.

What we lack in talent must be compensated with courage.

It is paradoxical that we should democratically decide
that institutions should be undemocratic
as the only way to keep their independence.

I'm not mistaken,
what happens is that I have my own way of getting it right.

The good thing about being surrounded by imbeciles
is that you can excel by comparison.
This is especially useful
when working in an organization.

What makes some societies unfeasible
is that structurally crime pays.

Some people, when having faith in their country
count with everything, but their countrymen.

America, all of it, is the sum of disunities.

A gift is to give someone
something he or she cannot do for himself.

To do what was not needed is no deed but waste.

We tend to pay more attention
to everything that tends to confirm our suspicions.

Nothing can beat the charm of the plain and simple.
Unfortunately, the reality is far from it.

Simplicity in the law discourages corruption and inefficiency.

I do not advocate universal truths,
not so much because they are non-existent
but especially because they are obstacles
to the development of new ideas.

Certain passports only lead to discrimination.

The worst villain is one who thinks that the circumstances
fully justify his or her behaviour.

People worry of the cost of things
but they do not stop to understand
that the true cost comes from not having them
and not being able to enjoy them.

Socialism begins with populist rhetoric
with a futile wind of hope
to finally perch on a ration card.

The stupidity spreads like a virus.

It is not that age makes better negotiators.
What happens is that time has allowed them to make more mistakes
and hopefully learn from them.

Some confidence verges on unconsciousness,
almost like the confidence of neonates towards their parents.

The inadequates will end up leaving us with no rights,
since society, rather than doing something specific with these,
believes it is better to punish everyone.

Sometimes I just prefer rumours;
facts may be misleading!

We must be able to recognize the virtue of silence.

Journalists should treat the news with respect
to make it as clear and objective as possible.

In all truth;
the best thing about work and studies are the vacation periods.

2009

II. Wanderings

Being brave does not mean not being afraid
but despite of it, taking the risk to achieve the objectives.

There is nothing more unnatural than equality.

Even with the enemies we have to be honest
to indicate to them that they are.

The best of any trip is coming home.

The most dangerous person
is one who has nothing to lose.

Spiritual poverty can be overcome,
and certainly material poverty as well, once you are conscious
that it is not necessary for things to go badly for the others
in order for things to go well for you.

The TV and the Internet are teachers always willing to educate.
Not to be so much concerned about the availability as for the content.

The problem is not that we do not learn,
but that we learn too slowly.

It is not that few things bother me,
what happens is that I allow few things to bother me.

To strictly enforce the law
regardless of its spirit
results in the civilization's decadence
and an affront to the most basic intelligence.

I do not know how intelligent people
bear the nonsense done and said by the fools.

Disobeying before an unjust law
is indication of civility.

Politics duty to be is the art of the possible,
however in practice
it becomes the art of promising the impossible.

It is not life that disappoint us
but people and their behaviour.

Human misery is built by the hands of the inept.
These hands are surprisingly numerous and diligent.

It is worrying that throughout human history
there has been much more injustice than justice.

Maybe the only things you own are your thoughts.

It appears to be better an imperfect democracy
than a promising totalitarianism.

I do not always understand you,
but I always love you.

Our dreams evolve
faster than us.

Nature does not care about intelligence,
its only task is survival.

We are
what we do.

The poor do not understand that they will be even poorer
if they elect the demagogue.

There is nothing easier
than finding someone to fight.

The good political practice
consists not in the depth of the analysis
but on the basics of economic arithmetic.

We all end up detesting the alarm clock.

Nature is the least democratic and egalitarian.

Stupidity is contagious.
On the contrary, there are many people immune to intelligence.

Hope is our only choice.

How much of the bureaucracy and excessive control
is due to the dishonesty of the inadequate.

Nothing is further from the reality than the duty to be of things.

Memories are life.

Being prudent does not mean being fearful
while taking unnecessary risks
abuts with the nonsense.

Politics is not only knowing what you want,
but mainly understanding what the way is
and how to do it. Usually, politicians only
focus on the common places
of what is wanted and never the how,
that is why every time we are further from the duty to be of things.

I still have faith in the future of humanity
because there are exceptional and stubborn people
determined on doing good.

From hurrying
only accidents and bad businesses remain.

Politics are besieged by opportunism.

Truth has no contemplations.

In some countries, everything happens
and nothing happens.

Telling the story right is more important than the story itself.

Authority, per se, tends to be incompetent.

Giving authority to those who have never had it
usually instantly generates
authoritarian people without any criteria.

If the state insists on making laws for morons
it is encouraging citizens to behave as such.

The city chaos and its mortal traffic
is the result of idiots and morons.
I'm not saying there are no inept people elsewhere,
what happens is that here, not only did we get the majority,
but also the most selfish.

In matters of leadership,
many speak and few rolled up their sleeves.

For an authority to be respected
the first thing is that it has criteria. An authority without criteria,
not only is silly itself
but exerts injustice per se.

Life is difficult because of the constant change,
which is a fact; accept it.

Selfishness is not only vile in its foundation,
but ends up destroying who wields it.

What people think as useful spending
is often simply wasteful.

Behaviours are choices.

Perfect practice makes perfect,
same as bad practice makes disasters

Behaviours are neither good nor bad;
they are appropriate or inappropriate. Bottom line:
they are effective or ineffective.

Having a strategy,
any strategy,
is invaluable in the long term.

Leaders should be in the business of making good people better.

The use of logic
damages relationships.

At the end of the day,
it is how much love you carry in your heart;
and how much you have in your pocket.

The citizen's short memory
forgets who has built the homeland and elects demagogues.

Who,
if not the citizen is responsible for his or her government?

What saves humanity
is its innate ability to surprise and propose.

The truth is what we do.

After the invention of the wheel and the sail
globalization was inevitable.

The formation of a leader
is a long term process.

In politics, winning by a narrow margin,
is losing.

Good service
creates value instantly.

To have an accident and survive is not a feat,
the feat is not to have an accident.

To the extent that educators are able to leave
earlier memories in the minds of children
these will be able to be more intelligent
than their predecessors.

A society is lost and unbind
when yesterday's criminals are today's moralists.

The imbeciles do not realize that sometimes they are useful
to those who they were trying to do harm.

Talking about peace is easy when in front of you
is not he or she who causes the aggression.

Who does not appreciate his or her freedom,
not only does not deserve it,
but is very close to losing it
because of the inadequates.

There is nothing more useless than misdirected
good will efforts.

Over time I realized
that the best thing I have is my family and friends.

When you cannot criticize justice´s rules
it is a sign that it is neither just nor balanced.

There are inept people that believe
that speeches solve problems.

War is the worst plague,
wherever it comes from and for whatever motives.

With imposition;
not even heaven.

Our destiny is to be in motion.

A people without education
is a breeding ground for opprobrium dictatorships.

Journalists should be tranquil and objective.

Democracy has generated a false illusion of equality
putting aside reality, that fortunately,
we are all different.

There are individuals who do not make more mistakes
simply because of time restriction.

A pusillanimous judge is worse than a corrupt one.

A bad boss
insubordinates his or her subordinate.

Only the ones being led can recognize leadership.

When you are clear about the goal,
the path becomes easier ...
and the other thing to do is to insist, insist, and insist ...

Luck and scoring over time
are the fundamental components of politics.

It is a fact:
Like it or not,
we all make mistakes.

It is the right person
when being with that person
makes you the best you can be.

The judges rule in abstract
and senators legislate in abstract,
and in practice these are all abstract arguments
with bloodily real consequences.

Prohibition does not create a country of virtue
but a nation of delinquents.

People do not understand
that they can not make decisions
for things which consequences
they are not responsible.

Politics is everything.
The key is to show more
even if that means doing less.

Give somebody a PC
and they will start to create more work for others
than really solving the problems that need to be solved.

If there is no reliable information,
speculation will take its place.

Problems are not puzzles anymore;
they appear to be more of a mystery.
And mysteries have many solutions and possibilities.

The flaw with USA's service is that good service does not mean,
asking over and over if something is good.
Because annoying the customer is bad service.

The sum of happy days is what makes a happy life.

The only requirement to be a journalist
is to be an ignorant.

The people that exchange their freedom
by a dictator's promises of well-being
says goodbye to their freedom and buries its well-being.

To make your own hell
no help from anyone is required.

Life is about learning to negotiate with others and also with you.
For life is a continuous and endless negotiation.

Politicians are always doing what they are supposed to do;
focusing the responsibility on someone else
rather than themselves.

You remember best
what you did wrong.

One of the secrets to happiness
is to have someone clean and organize
the mess that one leaves behind.

The best thing anyone can do for the people they love
is to take care of their own health.

The important thing is to be making new mistakes
and not the same old ones.

Leadership is defined
through actions.

A good job rests in having a good leader.

When looking for a job
people should actually be looking for a good leader,
not just a role.

If anything is repairable it is shame.

Only God can stop a human being
with a cause in his or her heart.

For the developing countries not only would it be convenient,
but cheaper,
to take all its citizens
to visit the countries of the first world
in order to teach them that the basic rules of behaviour
make life in the cities less chaotic and unbearable.

It is exasperating and exhausting
the time lost in the anarchic traffic
and queuing to do unnecessary bureaucratic processes.

The crisis is learning's best catalyst.

In terms of infrastructure
we must only believe in the bulldozer's dialectic.

The bandit and his or her misdeeds sicken,
but what sickens most is society's indolence to these.

The generality is that everything is particular.

No one is a good judge of himself.

A society is lost in its foundation
if for the average citizen it is a better prize
to screw another than to win.

Individual freedom is always the first casualty in any war.
The worst part is how people applaud their loss
in the name of pseudo democracy.

Nothing more intolerant and dictatorial
than communist regimes and their advocates.

The writer does not justify, just writes.
Who justifies is the reader.

We failed as a society because we do not have
a vision of future, much less shared values.
And if such values exist they are neither rewarded nor recognized.

Citizens praise populist governments
without finding out that soon they will be under the yoke
of an absolutist state.

Legislating about the essential
does not seem to be a priority of the senates of the republics.
Only the clerical calls their attention.
Even more grave
is that the courts compete with the senates.

If focus on the fundamental is not a piece of business for the society
nor its congress, judges, government or journalists;
the evils are secured.

Do not be surprised of the results
if you leave the task
in the hands of incompetents.

Taking away people's time
is stealing their life.

The convenient thing of smiling,
is that the day that you do not do it
at least people will ask what is wrong.

It is not that we change,
what happens is that we become older.

We grow old
the day that our body and health
do not respond to what we want to do.

What others remember about us, is not us,
but what their memories remember.

The problem of bad customs
is they become a custom.

I always forgive,
what happens is that I remember and become angry.

One should only own that which one loves.

Love is the ultimate responsibility.

Youth gives us a sense of immortality.

The path to knowledge
cannot be martyrdom.

Justice is not only the first piece of business,
but the foundation of any society.

The only thing popular in the regimes that proclaim being popular
is injustice and misfortune.

The power of reason
is the weakest of all.

Absolute definitions do not exist;
they should always be subject to analysis.

Ignoring the substantive to focus on the trivial
is the root cause of misfortune.

History always grants another opportunity to individuals.
Nobody, not only is not a prophet in his or her own land,
but in his or her time.

Selling hope to people is the best business.

The citizen who does not participate,
does not understand that at the expense of his or her children's welfare,
corruption feeds voraciously.

Violence has as its cohort corruption,
inefficiency and chaos.

The soldier is his or her honour.

That the good citizens
end up paying with their time and resources
all that the inadequates do
undermines the purpose of a society.

We must encourage people to read, even if it is our own.

Peace should be its own reward.

Peace and progress are not achieved with rhetoric.

Mine is definitely not to stop insisting.

Happiness is a life choice.

History and science are provisional
because as new evidence is known
these evolve.

The problem of history is that it is never told entirely.

Society does not understand that succumbing to the inadequates,
not only generates more
but eliminates the few freedoms of the just.

Repeating the argument does not improve it.

Lead is to propose and act.

We are victims of our own reality.

Nothing better to laugh than the antics said
by populist politicians. And it would really be funnier
if unfortunately they were not true intentions.

Unable to mitigate the danger,
it is best to ignore it completely.

Democracy is the opposite of the electoral unanimity.

There is nothing more brief than a State policy.

The totalitarian when seeking power,
are the first to say
that there is never enough free speech
to propose their thesis. Once in power,
are the first to eliminate all freedoms from their opponents.

In search of non-existent equality, society
increases inequality
when giving priority to a few.

Typically, men begin
to rely more on God when they marry.
Not to mention when they become parents.

Addictions
steal our freedom.

It is not life that has meaning,
it is the human being who gives meaning to life.

What to us rarely requires explanation,
for others it is almost incomprehensible.

In the lives of others
we usually are judges
instead of witnesses
and vice versa to our own.

Much accuracy
leads to inaccuracy.

There is nothing easier than to ask forgiveness
when we do not feel guilty.

Happiness is to make someone happy
being happy doing it.

Curiosity is the greatest talent,
both constructive and destructive,
that the human being possesses.

Curiosity is the foundation
of creation and innovation.

As much as we believe so,
nagging does not repair the damage.

Life is choices.

People forget that brains and hearts
are always mobile.

They say that the human being
is capable of doing everything that he or she proposes:
That is exactly what worries me sometimes.

Leadership
is the ability to transform
oneself and the environment.

The tragedy of democracy is that citizens
are not aware of the cost
of choosing demagogues and tyrants.

With the quality of current journalism,
saying that the historian is history's journalist,
is not only unfair to the historian
but infamous with history.

We become what we think,
and our thoughts create our world.

We, the thinkers,
begin responding like automatons.

Get to the point...now!

Some people do not seem so bad
simply because we do not have them so close.

Life must be lived
with mixed feelings of joy and happiness.

An essential part of justice
is that it acts promptly.

Usually we only appreciate things in retrospect.

Life as it comes,
must always be taken with a good sense of humour.

You teach by example.

For good advice only common sense is required.

Crises are solved with astuteness, intelligence and reason.

Marriage means to forgive every day.

Listening is the first sign of compassion.

Surely we are not the source of all solutions,
so at least we should not be the source of all problems.

The demagogue has the same ability to govern
as the critic has to execute.

That you do not acknowledge that it is happening
does not mean it is not happening.

The problem with fears
is the fact that thinking too much about them turns them into reality.

Without reciprocity,
fidelity is not only unworthy to the recipient
but pathetic to whom grants it.

The problem of radicalism
is when radicalization turns against us.

Radicalization
is the sure way to bitterness.

It is sad that the worst of oneself
are the others.

Emergencies lay bare
the inadequacies and improvisations.

To live you learn living:
There is no substitute.

Constraints
are the source of creativity.

I would have liked that you had believed in me
especially when I did not believe in me.

Freedom is deserved
by who appreciates it.

It is a blessing to make happy
those who you love by
being just as you are.

The problem with war
is that it has no fixed term.

Thank you for being there
even when I am not.

I am happy because I want to,
not because of my circumstances.

Business is not about who your competition is.
It is all about understanding who your customer is
and satisfying its needs.

Some people act like the devil
within the devil.

If you are not capable of enjoying the journey,
the finish line is not deserved.

What a blessing
is being fundamentally happy.

When politicians only talk about the parochial
it is the journalism' obligation to insist
on the important issues of a country.
If both politicians and journalism
are solely interested in the parochial,
the country is lost.

Everyone is not only responsible
but the author of his or her own happiness.

The question to the meaning of life is to be answered
with actions and not words.

The ability to be happy is something,
which fortunately
can be learned.

Accidents are often the form in which the unconscious
makes a reality
of the excuses.

I will stop asking; you think?

Many forget
that neither health nor time
can be stored.

I want to make you happy
being happy.

2010

III. Passages

Generosity is always the best path.

Bad taste is something best left for privacy.

The fact of learning to live in the present
keeps us from the fears of the past and the future.

Where there is more
also there is the least.

We should pay more attention
to what is not said
than to what is said.

Defending those who defend democracy and the rule of law,
and therefore defend us,
is the least by reciprocity and vital for survival.

The natural and obvious is that no place
should be forbidden for a good citizen.

The aim of totalitarian states
when trying to destroy the family unit
is to individualize the entire population
so that it becomes an amorphous mass.

We are often not conscious
of how important we are to other people.

The path and its challenges
is what makes the hero.

No one can be unhappy having health and friends.

If there is something which has real social impact
it is the construction of infrastructure.

The true leader and teacher
is one who teaches others
to think for themselves
and develop their own criteria.

You are
what you give.

Perform instead of idealizing.

Defend things
while they are still defendable.

It is essential to understand if something is aid or obstacle.

The only meaning in life is to be happy
making happy the people we care for.

In a family who need to be better educated
are the parents.

The best manager is a good mother.

Maturity is to be responsible for yourself.
And being responsible is caring diligently for your whole being.

Things are usually easy to say and difficult to do.

Globalization is the hero, not the villain
of the epic struggle against poverty.
The villain is and always has been corruption.

Theocracies would have us believe
that the pseudo prophets are wiser than God.

To really ban something,
it has to be prohibited
throughout its entire supply chain,
otherwise it generates value to the riskier links
and society would be better off legalizing it.

Given the state's inability
to enforce the most essential laws,
it chooses to make more laws.
As if making laws would generate their compliance.

No one can make anyone happy
if first he or she is not happy with himself.

Of course, living is risky,
but if you do not want the risk the answer is simple.

Ideas belong to whom executes them.

The city of today is a worthy mirror
of its rulers' competencies.

As human beings, the natural thing would be
that we did not allow human rights' violation.

It is always more valuable and important
to anticipate than react.

Living history is not the same as understanding it.

Laws are made for angels
forgetting our humanness.

The attachment to the extremes generates suffering.

What differentiates the developed countries to which are not,
are not their problems, but their solutions.

The instrument
should not be allowed to take possession of its owner.

A leader calls to reflection and to action.

An error is not fixed with another.

The truth should
neither surprise nor offend.

Happiness is not just an individual responsibility
but a social duty.

The important thing is not who said it
but if one understands it.

Those who think they are more are the ones who are less.

For security to be a social good
requires that state forces
take care of everyone equally
and not that most resources are destined
to take care of a few.

Respecting the truth is to respect justice.

Inexperience of new parents
makes life even more miraculous.

Communism hates progress, freedom,
economic development and good governance
because they all show its incompetence and demagoguery.

The first thing is to be certain of your uncertainties.

When developed countries
watch the developing countries
they usually forget that not long ago
they were worse off
because of wars and tragedies.

All nations were equally savage at some time.

Are these other times and have we learned from past mistakes?
Neither the first, nor much less the latter.

Denying the truth does not eliminate it.

The demagogue rejoices at the sight of perpetuating misery
because it is the way to get the gullible electors
to continue to believe in their false promises.

A state that is unable to protect its people,
is not even a state.

The citizen almost always knows where the dangers are,
unlike the authorities for whom everything
is a mystery.

The success of any relationship
lies in how aligned
are the tastes and interests of the parties.

Of the most expensive
is passivity.

The individual egoism
generates collective submissiveness.

Forgetting human nature and its consequences
is not only useless but clumsy.

Humanity is neither the best
nor the worst of its individuals.

One of the root causes of underdevelopment,
is that people prefer to stop having
provided the others are denied from having.

What the government fails to understand
is that prohibitions create
excellent business opportunities for crooks.

In politics it never goes out of fashion the lack of focus
on the real problems and their solutions.

When judges sentence differently for the same act
it is a symptom of injustice.

With one or two senses that are filled up,
everything seems more prodigious.

With love and desire anything is possible.

Happiness is the journey.

People are not fed neither by speeches nor promises.

The gullible elector does not understand that his or her pocket
and through the sacrifice of his or her children's future
the promises made by the populist politician will be paid.
The sad thing is that the money is spent
without making the promises a reality.

In too many occasions there are actions without consequences.

As in progress the least significant is the past,
the demagogue politician focuses strongly on it.

For anyone it is a tranquillity
to be surrounded with people who tell the truth.

I think that the world should get used to
listening to the truth.

Actions define a human being.

The progress, justice and security,
while they are political goods,
are far from being owned by a party.
Usually the demagogue parties
claim the authorship.

We would be happier if the individual problems
would have anonymous solutions.

The priority of a leader
is to train his or her replacement.

The problem of politicized justice
is that for the same act some are sentenced
while others rewarded.

What a happiness is life
with the hope that grants the power to make happy
who you love being just as you are.

Use what you have learned in life to have a better life.
Do not just ignore it.

In life you have to get rid of obsessions
to become freer.

Organizations are a mix
of the incongruence of goals and the struggle for power.

The best gifts
are those that can be shared.

If in a relationship one party is the one that always cedes,
then it is not a good relationship.

A better world is built enjoying full freedom
with full responsibility.

When deciding it is just as important what is done
as what is left behind.

The happiness that comes from having a bad memory
is unequalled.

One thing is the social obligation to help the unprotected,
and other, having to finance the irresponsible and corrupt.

Mirrors
are eyes that forget.

I am convinced that things
should be done only in a way;
the best way.

Trying to change the essence is not only an error
but impossible.

The penalty is part of the education.

Bad education is always of bad receipt and result.

People want and need to be governed
by true executives and not political parties.

I am fortunate to be understood
by the intelligent readers.

The best thing of being me is having you.

All the nations and individuals clamour for freedom,
the first freedom to be claimed
is to be freed from our own foolishness.

A more peaceful and harmonious society
would cost much less and would be of great value,
especially for our grandchildren.

Society is lost
when no one feels the hurt of stagnation
and lack of progress.

People conclude without being coherent
with the consequences of such conclusion.

When justice is not such,
the motherland is non-existent.

As I write,
I forget.

Sincerity does not protects us from unhappiness.

People say what they say
because of who they are.

Of what we are less innocent
is of our feelings.

Instead of choosing whom to save them,
the people elect who takes them to the gallows.

The truer it is,
the more is despised by the silly.

Life and happiness
are its own motive and finality.

The most serious thing about silliness
is that it does not even raise doubts.

To act from self-consciousness results in self-care and future.

It seems obvious that we are the result of what we are and do.
What it is not obvious is the way we are conscious
of what we are and do.

We start to look like
the people and the environment we are surrounded by.

In a relationship,
the lack of interest of one is not compensated
by the great interest of the other.
Just as one's weaknesses
are not compensated by the strengths of the other.

There is no motherland
when no one identifies with anyone.

Justice is a farce
when inoperative principles are applied
to a chilling reality.

The effectiveness of a leader
resides in his or her capacity to integrate.

The journalist should inform truthfully.
Society expects the journalist
to be truthful before informing.

Happiness and the fulfilment of dreams
must be the compass rose of life.

At the end of the day, we do what we do,
so we are wanted a little more each day.

What a happiness
is to love
with total admiration.

When a nation is unable to enforce the law,
the populist politician and negligent judge
conclude that the problem must be the law.

Who fights for his or her happiness
deserves it.

For a nation to be one
the decisions of politicians and justice
must be as brave as the actions of its army.

We must always put goodwill to life.

Make me
alright
to you.

Part of the charm
is having flaws.

A theory claiming that a good ruler
should concentrate all powers,
fails in both premise and conclusion.

Inflation, insecurity and lack of opportunities
are even crueller on the poor people.
It is ironic that these same people are the ones that choose
demagogues who are responsible
of stripping them, everybody else and future generations of everything.

With love and patience everything is possible.

Intelligence is inversely proportional
to the ability to listen to stupidity.

The role of the journalist
is to make the public understand the interviewee,
not to destroy him.

Hurry
is contradictory to elegance.

The one that steals dreams
is as corrupt as the one that steals money.

It is very difficult to love someone
who does not want to be loved.

Balancing the load is in practice
to distribute wear evenly.

Is there another way to do things
but with all the enthusiasm and passion.

Before it was thought that both the Earth and the universe
were flat, none is.
Clearly the only flat thing
has been mankind's thinking.

War is not fought or won by law.

Grave when justice instead of judgments
issues press releases.

It is a feat not to be irritated by the lack of criteria.

The demagogue politician and the useless journalist
delight in the endurance capacity of the submissive people.

I respect the laws
that respect me.

Few understand the harm caused by ignorance.

Trying to escape fate
only seals it.

The human capacity to feel guilty is infinite.

We believe who agrees with us.
Who agrees with us already has
an essential part of our trust.

Justice tastes like heaven.

The problem is not whether things are given to the one that needs them
but really that almost never are they given to the one that deserves it.

The fundamental
is the best filter.

If you believe in me,
I believe more in me.

People who are idiots, let them be;
do not join them.

Ironic that the more serious a country's problems are,
the less serious its leaders are.

A leader is responsible for his or her people in good times
and especially in bad times.

If the judge does not know the reality he or she judges
his or her sentences will always be unjust.

With the jolts that occur in the progress policy,
more than often far worse errors are made
than the ones that are tried to correct.

He or she who expects nothing
is never disillusioned.

In order to have a happy and lasting marriage,
both people must really share the essential,
that which is as vital as the air they breathe.

It is important to understand the fundamental need
of vital personal space and time.

Success is a mixture of intelligence and purpose.
Lacking intelligence, good is purpose.

To generate innovation
it is not necessary to think about how to make the task more efficiently
but how to dissolve the fact of having to do it.

It is better to have been wrong for taking action
than to have been for inaction.

Those who have not been exposed to the realities
judge quickly.

The philosophy that the evils are not as infamous
as long others suffer them, is morally unacceptable.

Happy people are the only ones that can dream big.

We need to acquire
the vice of really being ourselves.

The taste and passion
are always more important than knowledge.

The only way for things to make sense
is arriving to reason through emotion.

Who thinks the worst rarely becomes disappointed.

You can measure the person by the accuracy of his or her words.

Biased justice cannot be a spectacle for anyone.

Before biased justices
the only way to prove the innocence
is by fleeing.

The structural inefficiency
can only be overcome with creativity.
Adding more resources to structural inefficiency
only prolongs it.

It is more valuable to recover a lost friend
than to make a new one.

Driving and football
tend to bring out the worst feelings in some human beings.

Who is in love
knows it as much as anyone knows that his or her heart beats.

When nothing neither fills nor compensates
the only answer is love.

Love, like happiness,
is its own means and its own end.

Love without desire
is less than a whim.

People do not even become aware
that being a better person
not only does it not cost more
but is very easy.

What is essential is the essential
and has no substitutes.

To learn
you have to keep the persistence of children.

Wise is who manages to fulfil his or her dreams.

People tend to be more liberal
offering than granting.

Insanity is not doing the necessary
to be happy.

The underlying problem always lies
in not asking the right questions.

Life is more enjoyable when you have someone to share it with.
And sharing it means that that person
shares your same essence.

Individual freedom is the source of progress.

It's amazing that the person you least expect
is the one that pulls out from you millions of smiles
when your soul feels off.

If you cannot find your place,
the more likely it is that your place
is yet more distant in time.

Pretending to escape your essence
is nothing more than foolishness.

Each of us is master and slave of our fears.

A fundamental part of a good decision
is that it is taken with opportunity.

We must prepare for the worst
and always hope for the best.

Informing, as well as complaining without proposing
is not only foolish but useless.

In creative hands, restrictions are the tools,
raw materials and the catalysts for innovation.

It is dangerous
to underestimate the clumsiness and futility
of the ignorant
and those lacking judgment.

The vast majority of life's aspects
have no choice but to be lived:
There is no explanation that teaches to live.

Gullible legislators and judges
do not understand that to prohibit without giving options
generates people to fail to comply with the prohibition.

Happiness is selfish.

Knowing someone too much
may jeopardize the relationship.

True wisdom
is to take appropriate actions
to make things happen.

Happiness is not a given,
it is yours to take.

If sometimes we have to be distant
from the opinions of those who cherish us,
with greater reason we have to so from those who do not.

Happiness comes
from within each individual.

It is better to err following the heart
than blindly follow reason and be right.

We must make decisions
from what we want.

The best thing you have in life
is yourself,
and the only thing.

We must enjoy and be delighted with the virtues we have.

What is not noticed is that it is not.

The happy person has the virtue of feeling the desire to be it
without any effort.

Each of us should be conscious of our virtues
and define ourselves in those terms.

Doubt yourself,
because it is your beliefs that have led you to where you are.

Decisions
can not be taken out of fear.

When trying to fill the emptiness
human beings make the worst mistakes.

When you have passion in life,
the body and soul neither become tired nor hurt.

The essential
is to find oneself.

Who sees only with his or her eyes
is easy to fool.

We tend to talk about what we believe.

Defending the intimate time with yourself
is essential to know yourself.

The family nucleus has the capacity
to be most enriching
or the most sickening to the individual.

In essence you get
what others grant.

Reality
is very distant to the duty to be.

A society in which the pardon
is directly proportional to the blood spilt
only rewards the violent
and punishes good citizens.

Things well done
are timeless.

Underdevelopment is aggravated because
specialists in finding problems emerge
rather than in finding solutions.

Wisdom
is the product of experience.

We should pay more attention to actions than words.
Reality is the actions, not the words.

Everything is in our hands,
the best and the worst.

We are not conscious
of what we overlook.

Being happy
is a task
daily and urgent.

When people do stupid things,
the punishment for all, is more regulations.
I believe we need less regulation, not more;
as well as we need people to be smarter, not dumber.

Regulations are not a guarantee
for anything.

Maturing is to become conscious of what really matters
and act accordingly.

In a democracy, the vote from the ignorant
is worth the same as the one from the thoughtful citizen.
The populist politician knows that convincing the ignorant
is his or her natural skill.

I do not know everything,
but at least I have accumulated some experience.

Everything should be tested through the perspective of time.

Sometimes the best way to avoid danger
is to postpone it.

I have no way and no intention to resist myself.
There is no point to it.

The populism recipe
has always been the same
and is dressed again and again as a progressive idea.
The unwary citizen does not understand
that this recipe is and only results in misery.

In this life the only obligations
are to be happy and not be an imbecile.

If age alone meant wisdom there will not be so many old cretins.

The selfishness of the average politician,
not only makes politics unfeasible
but especially the progress of society.

Ignorance of risk and danger
are a blessing to the silly.

Nothing like the conviction granted by ignorance.

Inefficiencies in private business
are the cause of bankruptcy,
in state business
they are a source of corruption.

Competitiveness does not depend on the size and resources:
depends on the initiative for innovation.

We cannot imagine
what is not in us.

Not exercising rights is losing them.

2011

IV. Along the Side of the Journey

Is not the words
but the actions that matter.

For every war it is always necessary an excuse.

Intelligence is doing the opposite
of what the mass does.

What we love rejuvenates us.

Responsibility is not only doing what we must,
but especially being careful and protecting yourself.

Who does not want to learn,
life takes charge in teaching him or her.

More than respect
we should seek to earn
the hope of others.

To be a judge, the main thing is to be fair,
knowing the law is not everything.

Thinking freely
has always been the most dangerous adventure for a human being.

Life is a journey
that everyone must walk by himself or herself.

The challenge of a leader, as well as of a teacher,
is to gain the attention of his or her people,
not force it.

The great advances of humankind have been possible
thanks to the courage to experiment and explore the new,
and almost always against the alleged right answers.

Neither bliss nor happiness
are chance.

Nothing is like the harmony and tranquillity
that grants being genuine and unpretentious.

You have to rely more on instinct than reason.

Authority tends to be exercised only
against good people.

People who have contact and affection with animals
tend to live longer.

Subsidies should be watched over,
since their misuse causes society
to end up promoting laziness and squandering.

Rest is to do what one really likes.

Nothing is like the safety we feel
when desired by the person we love.

The problem is not that politicians
tend to be obvious and bad liars,
but that the incautious voter believes them.

Innovators aren't often celebrated; not at first.

So much is often viewed as unnecessary.

To initiate a war any pretext is enough.
Peace requires almost all the arguments
and plenary justifications.

Old age does not grant neither good criteria nor maturity per se.
The only thing it does gives to someone that does not mature
is a problematic personality.

Aggression is often the primary resource
for those who are not right.

Good attitude is the quality of adaptable and capable people.

The secret of happiness
is to live our own essence.

It is grave when the state treats its citizens
as potential delinquents;
tragic when they really are.

While being honest has no incentives
and being corrupt has all,
structurally we cannot expect
neither better people nor a better society.

The duty to be
is that who has been honest
at least should pay less tax and make fewer cues,
not the opposite.

In organizations,
it is easier to guide and control lions
than dinosaurs.

A leader should always have more questions than answers.

The organizational absurd manifests its splendour
when its pseudo leaders impose their ignorance
on the knowledge and experience
of those who not only know
but are the ones doing the work.

To govern is to transform the present reality
and materialize a better future,
not simply promising.

The populist politician abhors
the legal and controlled exploitation of resources while
always looking the other way when this is done illegally.

Purity is a good mask for corruption
because it discourages inquiry.

Exposing corruption
challenges the very nature of what a society imagines it is.

Incentives work only with people that care enough for them.

The problem is not the ridiculous idea that communism is progressive
but populist politicians who considered it to be
the quintessential form of government.
Not to mention the gullible voters who believe it.

History has proven again and again that communism is
synonymous with atrocious dictatorships.
Of course, humankind never learns from its mistakes.

Success is the result of cumulative advantages.

Enriching criticism
is journalism's role.

It is not easy to solve ethical problems
due to the centrifugal pull of responsibilities
from all the different stakeholders.

Science is the result of asking essential questions
and pursuing passionately the answers.

The structural difference between individuals
and what we call talent; is the sum of advantages
or opportunities since early childhood.

Achievement is more about taking advantage of opportunities
than mere talent.

To talk about ethics in a general way is easy
because the contradictions of real life are absent from it.

We like to think that we are not prisoners of our past.

Success arises
from a predictable set of circumstances and opportunities;
it is not a random act.

A perfect life is next to impossible,
so as life without mistakes is not of much good either.

We believe that those working frantically in the cities
are making their living while actually they are losing their lives.

Each of us is and will be,
to a great extent,
what we have been.

The incompetent person is very clever
to create chaos and confusion,
and thus justify their role.

Once elected, the corrupt and populist politicians,
impose their will
fleeing plural and democratic debate
that when being candidates they so much advocated.

The problem of aesthetics
is that everybody thinks they have good taste.

Underdevelopment
is a legitimate son of a country's chronic improvisations.

History is compelling in demonstrating
that the left has never guaranteed democracy,
what has evidently always guaranteed
is authoritarianism and subjugation of the people
at the hands of despots and dictators.
And leftists despots and dictators, believe with all faith,
that because they are leftists there not despots nor dictators.

It seems that the left
is only capable of producing dictatorships
with its traditional consequence of misery for all.

The founding fathers should work for the country
with a mother's abnegation.

Underdevelopment and misery
are the only recipes that the populist politician knows and applies.

The justice of a cause can be perceived
depending on who supports it.

As the most practical thing for bad leaders
is to avoid solving problems;
denial and wasting everybody's time eliminates their worries.

Great works for the betterment of humanity
have been made by own will
very few by obligation.

The truth is, that the truth
is nothing more than an interpretation of reality.

The right and what is necessary
is anything but democratic.

There are nations that are abstracted from the reality of globalization
and carve with delirious enthusiasm their underdevelopment.

The problem of such journalistic news burst
is that society fails to recover
when it is already flooded with more. Of course,
there is never posterior follow-up for constructive purposes.

We are the sum of our actions.

The truth is a process.

Do not fight always against the world
because the world usually wins.

The only way to improve the productivity of a company
is that all employees
begin to think more and 'work' less.
The activity does not add value per se.

Citizens should worry that the politician
does not make decisions based on society's sustainability
but with myopic electoral calculation.
This passivity of citizens to this reality
will be regretted by their grandchildren in the future.

Reality hits you bluntly in the face,
again and again.

You can tell a city's urban planning
by the amount of air wiring.

We seek perfection
in an imperfect world by nature.

Legislation is introduced for the occasion
rather than structurally.

Distrust is the most barren soil.
Where there is no trust nothing grows
and nothing can be built.

For an artist,
the only acceptable criticism
is the one coming from those
who have had the same job.

With violence, not only do victims lose,
but society has already lost the perpetrators from its herd.

Reality cannot be changed,
but its perception can.

Unlike intelligence,
ignorance let alone stupidity,
are unconscious of themselves.

Peace is something imposed by the victor
over the vanquished.

Life is the now and the future is present.

Dreams call destiny.

An essential value in a society
is the voluntary obedience of the rules.
The society that does not recognize this
is always on the verge of extinction.

The voluntary obedience of the rules is not a class issue,
after all the poor people
are the ones who suffer most when there is no civic culture.

Everything in life and the universe, luckily,
turns out to be more complicated.

The truth, the ugly truth,
is that we never possess anything but us.
And most of the time not even that.

Everyone should be the hero
of his or her own existence.

A country where there is only talk about banalities
rather than the substantive issues has no future.

To really solve problems, and especially their root causes,
it is necessary to use a distinctive approach.

Everything is easy once we understand it.

Leaders lead best when they supervise less.

No wonder companies are unrelated to science
when the only literature that employees consume
are emails with trifles.

Who does not work consciously
with the intention of promoting a prosperous neighbourhood
is seriously jeopardizing his or her future.

Knowledge without practice is not knowledge.

Politicians who only forbid
as a solution to all problems
lack imagination on the surface
and ultimately have a spirit of despots.

That justice
has authority to order preventive detention
without mediating judgment
is an absurdity in itself.

Unconsciously
we seek the unconscious that complement our unconscious.

To be absorbed in work
is the best anaesthesia
to avoid feeling the passage of time and life without living it.

For good parents,
the mere presence of their children makes them happy.

With good infrastructure any place is close,
achievable and enjoyable.
The politician sells infrastructure promises
to get votes without understanding the harm
it does to society when he or she fails.

The populist politician
does not understand that addiction to subsidies
poisons the progress and sustainability.

There is nothing more unnatural than what does not evolve.

It is grim that the circumstantial of a system is the structural.

Besides being daring,
ignorance is suspiciously brave.

You end up believing in something, even if it is not true,
just because it is useful.

I do not tolerate the intolerant.

If power has to be to proven
is because it is not have.

The one that thinks that by writing emails leads;
starts from a wrong assumption:
that people really read emails.

The populist politicians
still insist that words
are much better than actions to solve problems.
Unfortunately, problems need action to be solved
and reality is blunt about it.

Diplomacy is the most powerful of the weapons
when used wisely.

Diplomacy consists, especially
in how to say no
making the counterparty perceive it
as a better response to a yes.

Some are solely interested in demanding
the enforcement of the laws in their favour.

The error is even worse when you do not learn from it.

Fanaticism is always the first obstacle
in the search for truth.

Things start to be missed more
when they are possessed by another.

The consumer ends up paying
all the inefficiencies of the system.

The citizens elect leaders
who instead of offering solutions impose restrictions.
Whereupon the incautious electors
have increasingly fewer rights.

To evolve in life you have to learn
that the learned has to be unlearned.

For love it is possible to endure even the impossible.
But someone who makes you stand it clearly does not love you.

Attitude often is not only the most important thing
but the solely important thing.

It has no future a society
that believes that honest success, creation,
talent and difference
must be punished.

A dictator's main strategy,
to gain power and perpetuate in it,
is to rely on the working class
who are certainly the majority,
for which not only they polarize society
but squandered with delirious enthusiasm public money,
product of those who pay taxes,
in punctual aids
instead of in structural solutions.

Rights are rights;
Not to be supplicated nor begged.

History has shown
that people who are generous and unsuspecting
with the left
always await yokes, miseries and dictatorships.

As the politician does not know reality
supposes that deforming it is enough.

The populist leader,
rather than devote himself to work in depth
to resolve issues,
dedicates his or her time to make speeches and give interviews
in which his or her fertile imagination
leads him to believe he or she does a magnificent job.
And the useless journalist plays along
without criticizing.

The left never promotes
the middle and lower classes who they claim to represent,
let alone it does not believe in consensus nor cultivated knowledge,
all critics are a nuisance.

Exercising humility
is the only thing capable of counteracting
the disturbance that power produces.

The populist leader invents problems where there are solutions.
So, not only satisfies his or her ego
but leaves the real issues intact.

2012

The problem with democracy
is that it obliges to elect
between the corrupt and the inept.

The populist leader blames everyone
but his or her improvisational mania and ineptitude,
of whatever goes wrong.

As a member of an organization,
worry about your behaviours,
if your colleagues do not want to invite you
to your own farewell party.

Two bad businesses
do not make a good one.

Mediocrity is corruption's legitimate child.

Usually the weight of a satrap
is inversely proportional to the minions he or she has around
to ensure a poor servile court,
of which he or she only expects blind obedience.

If you can figure out what motivates people
you can understand their behaviours.

As in every epoch,
public opinion is easily deceived.

Money problems
are often the ones with the easiest solution.

The most idiot
is the idiot's seconder.

Authorities believe that by limiting citizens' rights
they are protecting them.
The incredible part is that people believe it;
the common good may be just a mirage.

The real inequality
is that for some everything is required
meanwhile everything is tolerated from others.

Politics should not be ruled
by emotion nor passion but by reason.

An artist can start to feel successful
when he or she starts to be copied.

The exercise of democracy results
in one of increasingly complex manipulation.

The socialist politician is successful
in his or her endeavour to privatize the state to usufruct it,
while he or she makes the citizen believe
that he or she is waging a social battle.

It seems that the only way to achieve peace
is winning the war with forcefulness.

Mankind has always been the owner
of its own
demons and fears.

The irresponsible journalist
is primarily interested in the scandal
without even pausing to examine
the accuracy of its impugnment.

The search for peace can contain everything
but never the award for crime.

I do not know what is more dangerous,
the politician who fails to fulfil his or her promises
or the one that fulfils them.

The despot poses tolerant, while stigmatizing his or her critics.

Too bad that bosses in organizations
only believe in their people
when it suits them.

There are people who replace their lack of experience
with recklessness.

More work is required to be unhappy
than to be happy.

If history shows us anything,
is that evolution of humankind does not always
head in a positive direction.

The best efficiency formula
is to transform any process in unnecessary and irrelevant.

An essential part of maturing
is understanding that we are not islands
and we increasingly need further advice and support.

Good memories depend on what we live
and not on what others opine.

Hope is the vital force.

2013

Poems

Fortune
For Natalia

With you I have all possibilities
the possibility to be
And be
to submit to love
And be its hostage

With you I can be
decently indecent
respectfully disrespectful

I have the possibility to try
prying how would you look as a nonagenarian

so I covet
to increase the inventory of coincidences
to prove that
my destiny
and fortune
was finding you
So finally
I can see your eyes
in the reflection of mine
in yours.

2007

Premonitions

Finding you is my joy
moreover,
the value of wanting each other
in excess.

> "Marriage
> if it does not
> I will still
> I no longer

Discovering you is my reason for being
moreover,
refine our collection of
complicities.

Finding you is my life
moreover,
discovering every day in each
other.

Discovering each other is our prize
moreover,
keep our love
and have all the time and health in the world
to care for each other
and license from God to love us without
distractions
achieve an extraordinary and affine future
moreover,
dialogue with humour in all
instances and moments
and beg to the sky the treasure of enjoying
holding our grandchildren in our arms
moreover,
meet the final date,
together.

does not mean anything, mean this:
love you when
love you."
Adler

Together
meet the final date,
moreover,
holding our grandchildren in our arms
and beg to the sky the treasure of enjoying
dialogue with humour in all
instances and moments
moreover,
achieve an extraordinary and affine future
keep our love
to care for each other
and license from God to love us without
distractions
have all the time and health in the world
moreover,
discovering each other is our prize.

Discovering every day in each
other,
moreover,
finding you is my life.

Refine our collection of
complicities,
moreover,
discovering you is my reason for being.

The value of wanting each other
in excess,
moreover,
finding you is my joy.

Premonitions

2008

Dream

We have what everybody wants
happiness and tranquillity.

Your dream
is my dream
My dream
is your dream.

And most importantly
our dream
is ours.

2008

For you

Mine is madness already,
madness for you
because I think of you
and miss you
in all moments
and also
between moments.

2008

Reasons

The reasons
are many,
the reason is one:
you stopped loving me.

2011

A Rose

A rose is a rose
but my rose is not any
mine is special
delicate by nature

It is a dream
My dream
It is true
It is real

Haughty in its beauty
has no equal
extraordinary in its own way
sensual her whole being

I dream with her
incites my being
I need her kisses
and to feel her skin.

2012

Contents

Acknowledgments 9
Foreword by Carlos Esteban Orozco Posada 13

Introduction 15

Thoughts and Reflections 19

I. Paths 21
II. Wanderings 37
III. Passages 59
IV. Along the Side of the Journey 83

Poems 105

Fortune 107
Premonitions 108
Premonitions 109
Dream 110
For you 111
Reasons 112
A Rose 113

www.ingramcontent.com/pod-product-compliance
Lightning Source LLC
Chambersburg PA
CBHW060816050426
42449CB00008B/1679